I0814872

OLYMPIC SPORTS

OLYMPIC SWIMMING

BY CHRÖS McDOUGALL

SportsZone
An Imprint of Abdo Publishing
abdobooks.com

abdobooks.com

Published by Abdo Publishing, a division of ABDO, PO Box 398166, Minneapolis, Minnesota 55439.

Printed in the United States of America, North Mankato, Minnesota.
102024
012025

Cover Photo: Maddie Meyer/Getty Images Sport/Getty Images
Interior Photos: Simon M. Bruty/Anychance/Getty Images Sport/Getty Images, 5; Ezra Shaw/Getty Images Sport/Getty Images, 6; Al Bello/Getty Images Sport/Getty Images, 9, 13; Greg Wood/AFP/Getty Images, 10; Petr David Josek/AP Images, 12; De Agostini Picture Library/Getty Images, 15; Topical Press Agency/Hulton Archive/Getty Images, 17; Scanpix Historical/TT News Agency/Alamy, 18; Bain News Service/Library of Congress, 21; Adam Pretty/Getty Images Sport/Getty Images, 22–23, 36, 41; Bettmann/Getty Images, 25, 27; Getty Images Sport/Getty Images, 29; Rich Clarkson/Rich Clarkson & Associate/NCAA Photos/Getty Images, 30; Gerry Cranham/Offside/Getty Images, 33; Kyodo/AP Images, 35; David J. Phillip/AP Images, 39; Ian MacNicol/Getty Images Sport/Getty Images, 40; Jonathan Nackstrand/AFP/Getty Images, 42; DBM/Insidefoto/Mondadori Portfolio/Getty Images, 44; Maddie Meyer/Getty Images Sport/Getty Images, 45

Editor: Haley Williams
Series Designer: Karli Kruse

Library of Congress Control Number: 2024938353

Publisher's Cataloging-in-Publication Data

Names: McDougall, Chrös, author.
Title: Olympic swimming / by Chrös McDougall
Description: Minneapolis, Minnesota: ABDO Publishing, 2025 | Series: Olympic sports | Includes online resources and index.
Identifiers: ISBN 9781098295516 (lib. bdg.) | ISBN 9798384916512 (ebook)
Subjects: LCSH: Olympic games--Juvenile literature. | Swimming--Juvenile literature. | Olympians (Olympic athletes)--Juvenile literature. | Olympics--History--Juvenile literature. | Sports--Juvenile literature.
Classification: DDC 797.2--dc23

TABLE OF CONTENTS

CHAPTER 1
THE CHASE FOR EIGHT 4

CHAPTER 2
OLYMPIC SWIMMING THROUGH THE YEARS 14

CHAPTER 3
SETTING THE STANDARD 24

CHAPTER 4
NEXT-LEVEL SWIMMING GREATS 34

GLOSSARY 46
MORE INFORMATION 47
ONLINE RESOURCES 47
INDEX 48
ABOUT THE AUTHOR 48

CHAPTER 1

THE CHASE FOR EIGHT

Michael Phelps drove his arms out in front of him, then thrust them back alongside his body. With each enormous butterfly stroke, the 23-year-old from Baltimore propelled himself forward through the water. After the first two laps, he held an early lead in the men's 400-meter individual medley (IM). But teammate Ryan Lochte and Hungary's László Cseh remained right at his side.

Phelps had arrived at the 2008 Olympic Games in Beijing, China, as the world's best swimmer. He had raced in his first Olympics at 15 years old in 2000 in Sydney, Australia. Four years later, in Athens, Greece, he tied the record for most medals in a single Olympics with eight. And six of those medals were gold. But in Beijing, Phelps had his eyes on something bigger. Thirty-six years earlier, fellow American swimmer Mark Spitz had won a record seven gold medals at the 1972 Olympics in Munich, West Germany. Phelps set out in Beijing to win eight.

At the 2000 Games, 15-year-old Michael Phelps became the youngest male athlete to represent Team USA at the Olympics since 1932.

Many people consider the butterfly to be the most difficult stroke in swimming.

He first had to win the 400-meter IM, though. Perhaps the sport's most grueling race, the 400 IM requires swimmers to use a different stroke every two laps. Phelps led after the 100 meters of the butterfly. Next up was the backstroke, which was Lochte's specialty. By the turn, Lochte had taken the lead. He was neck and neck with Phelps as the swimmers started the breaststroke leg. Phelps needed to make a move.

At 6 feet, 4 inches tall with a huge wingspan, Phelps had a body built for swimming fast. Pushing and pulling his long limbs through the water, he passed Lochte. And with each stroke, that lead grew. By the time Phelps launched into the closing freestyle leg, he was in command of the race. In the end, nobody finished within a body length of the American superstar. Phelps's time of 4:03.84 smashed his own world record by 1.41 seconds. And his quest for a record eight Olympic gold medals was on.

A GRUELING JOURNEY

Phelps faced his next big test just one day later. On August 11, he led off the 4x100-meter freestyle relay in American record time. But Australian Eamon Sullivan was even faster. Sullivan's world-record swim put his team in front. From there, all Phelps could do was wait.

Garrett Weber-Gale gave Team USA the lead in the second leg. But in the third leg, Fréd Bousquet of France pulled ahead. Many people expected France to win the race, including the French swimmers. They had the fastest time in the world that year, along with a superstar anchor in Alain Bernard. He dove in for the last leg with a half-second lead. By the turn, that lead had grown. With President George W. Bush looking on, Phelps's quest for history appeared over after just one win.

Then, something unexpected happened. Eying his opponent on each breath, Team USA's Jason Lezak began swimming faster and faster. With each stroke, the 32-year-old moved that much closer to Bernard. By the last 10 meters, they were practically even. It all came down to an all-out sprint to the finish. Fans inside Beijing's "Water Cube" arena rose to their feet. Stretching, Lezak reached the wall just .08 seconds ahead of Bernard. Phelps flexed and roared from the pool deck. In one of the most remarkable performances of all time, Lezak dropped the fastest relay split in history to secure another world record and keep Phelps's hopes for eight gold medals alive.

The dramatic finish electrified the crowd in Beijing. It also captured the attention of fans back home in the United States. Phelps's races became must-see events. And with each new win, that interest only grew.

On August 12, Phelps raced his third final. No one was close this time as he took nearly a second off the world record in the 200 freestyle. Two finals awaited on August 13. Midway through the 200 butterfly, water began leaking into Phelps's goggles. Nonetheless, he powered through the second half to hold off Cseh and set another world record. A half hour later, Phelps was back in the pool for the 4x200 freestyle. The Americans beat their own world record by nearly five seconds. They beat second-place Russia by even more.

Through five days of competition, Phelps had already raced 10 times, including preliminaries. After racing only prelims on August 14, he was back for another final on August 15.

About 4.7 billion people worldwide tuned in to the 2008 Games, which is the largest television audience ever for an Olympics.

And once again, he finished first. This time he easily held off Cseh to win the 200 IM while also setting another world record. With two events to go, Phelps's quest remained on track. However, his biggest test was on its way.

Phelps was coached for most of his career by Bob Bowman. They began training together at the North Baltimore Aquatic Club in Maryland when Phelps was 11 years old.

AN EPIC CLASH

Phelps had already made history in Beijing. His win in the 200 butterfly had given him 10 career gold medals. No athlete in Olympic history, in any sport, had that many. But the record everyone wanted to see was still to come. With a win in the 100-meter butterfly on August 16, Phelps could tie Spitz with seven gold medals in a single Olympics.

Seemingly everyone wanted to see Phelps do it. But not Milorad Čavić. Prior to the Olympics, the Serbian swimmer declared that Phelps was beatable. And Čavić wasn't alone in thinking that. Many people saw the 100 butterfly as Phelps's biggest challenge in Beijing. It was his shortest individual race. It also came late in the program. That meant his top opponents, with much lighter schedules, would enter the race a lot fresher. Čavić stoked the flames further after posting the fastest time in the semifinals. He said it would be good for the sport if Phelps lost.

BEST OF THE BEST

Michael Phelps won six medals, four of them gold, at the 2012 Olympics in London, England. However, it was not a happy experience for him. He was struggling with mental health. By his final Olympics in 2016 in Rio de Janeiro, Brazil, Phelps was in a better place. Cameras followed his wife and three-month-old son cheering him on. And they had plenty to cheer about. With five gold medals and a silver, Phelps ended his career with 28 medals, 23 of them gold. Both are all-time Olympic records.

All eyes were on the rivals in the final. Čavić took his place in lane four, with Phelps to his left in lane five. Then the 6-foot-5, 200-pound Čavić burst off the block. He planned to go out so hard that no one could catch him. Halfway through the race, that looked to be the winning strategy. Čavić had the lead at the turn, with Phelps more than a half-second back in seventh. But Phelps pushed hard off the wall. One by one, he overtook his opponents. With just a few meters to go, only Čavić remained in front of him.

Čavić stretched his arms and glided toward the wall. Phelps decided to sneak in one more half-stroke. To many people in the arena, it appeared Phelps had fallen short. Then the results flashed on the scoreboard. Phelps had edged Čavić by just 0.01 seconds. The Serbian team unsuccessfully protested the result. For the first time in a Beijing final, Phelps missed out on a world record. But he had tied Spitz's record.

The last step was breaking that record with a win the next day in the 4x100 medley. Most people expected Team USA to win. After two legs, the Americans trailed Japan and Australia. Then Phelps, swimming the butterfly, removed any doubt.

Although Phelps, *front*, didn't achieve a world record in the men's 100-meter butterfly at the 2008 Games, he did set an Olympic record.

From left, Phelps, Brendan Hansen, Jason Lezak, and Aaron Piersol show off their gold medals after winning the men's 4x100 medley relay at the 2008 Olympics.

His blazing third leg of the race put Team USA back into the lead. Lezak took it from there. Another speedy freestyle split secured Phelps his eighth gold medal and seventh world record of the 2008 Games. As Lezak touched the wall, an exhausted Phelps embraced his teammates. Finally, he raised both his arms into the air. After nine days and 17 races, Phelps had done it.

CHAPTER 2

OLYMPIC SWIMMING THROUGH THE YEARS

Historians believe people have been going into the water as long as there have been human beings. Records show that ancient Egyptians were swimming as early as 2500 BCE. Soldiers from both ancient Greece and Rome swam as part of their training for war. The first known swim races took place in Japan in 36 BCE.

However, swimming didn't begin to develop into the competitive sport that it is today until the mid-1800s. That proved to be good timing. During the late 1800s, a French educator named Pierre de Coubertin became inspired by the ancient Greek Olympics. In 1896, he organized the first modern Olympic Games. Athletes from 14 countries met that year in Athens. Swimming was among the nine sports contested there. Only swimming, fencing, gymnastics, and track and field have been in every modern Olympics.

The National Swimming Society was formed in 1837 in Great Britain. The organization started holding swimming competitions that year in London, England.

A LONG EVOLUTION

Today, swimming is one of the most popular Olympic sports. Athletes in high-tech swimsuits fly through the water. Competitions take place in brand-new 50-meter pools. Advanced timing systems clock the finishes to the hundredth of a second. None of this was the case at the 1896 Games.

The first Olympics included just four swimming races. Only men were allowed to compete. And all the events were held in the frigid Mediterranean Sea. Hungarian Alfréd Hajós won two of the races. He had hoped to win more. However, because all four events were held on the same day, he only raced the 100-meter and 1,200-meter freestyle.

Swimming moved to a pool for the 1908 Olympics in London, England. However, the pool was still outside, and it was built within the infield at the track-and-field stadium. It was also 100 meters long.

Over the years, familiar aspects of Olympic swimming were gradually introduced. The now standard 50-meter pool debuted in 1924 in Paris, France. Marked lanes were also introduced at those Games. The 1936 Olympics in Berlin, Germany, were the first to use starting blocks. Olympic swimmers first began racing under a roof in London in 1948. And competitors weren't allowed to wear goggles until the 1976 Games in Montreal, Canada.

Several sports were held outside in London's White City Stadium during the 1908 Olympics. Those included swimming, gymnastics, cycling, and wrestling.

WOMEN'S SWIMMING

Many sports were emerging and growing during the 1800s. However, these sports were almost exclusively for men. At the time, many people believed strenuous activity was harmful to women. As a result, women were not allowed to compete at the 1896 Olympics. Only a handful competed in the next three Games. But none of those women were swimmers.

That changed at the 1912 Olympics in Stockholm, Sweden. Even so, women still did not have the same opportunities as men. In 1912, only 27 women competed in swimming. And they were limited to two available events. That compared to 93 men who raced in seven events.

At the 1912 Games, women could compete only in the 100-meter freestyle and 4x100-meter freestyle relay events.

It took until 1996 for women and men to have the same number of swimming races at the Olympics. But they still didn't have the same events. The longest women's race was the 800-meter freestyle, whereas the men's long-distance freestyle race was 1,500 meters. Finally, at the Tokyo, Japan, Games in 2021, the program evened out. That year's Olympics added a women's 1,500 freestyle and men's 800 freestyle, finally giving men and women an equal number of events.

STROKES AND RACES

Olympic swim races are organized based on which stroke the swimmer can use. Freestyle swimming races have been held at every Olympics. In these races, swimmers can use any stroke. But because the front crawl is the fastest option, it is almost always used.

The first Olympic backstroke event took place at the 1900 Games in Paris. Eight years later, breaststroke joined the Olympic program. The newest Olympic swimming stroke is the butterfly. It didn't debut in the Games until 1956 in Melbourne, Australia. Today, men and women race in 100- and 200-meter events for each stroke at the Olympics. There are also 50-, 400-, 800-, and 1,500-meter freestyle races.

A fifth type of swim racing is called a medley. In these races, swimmers use each of the four strokes for a quarter of the race. The 400-meter IM for men and women was introduced to the Olympics at the 1964 Games in Tokyo. Today, men and women also race a 200-meter IM.

In addition to individual races, relays have been a part of Olympic swimming since 1908. In a relay, four athletes from a team

LOST EVENTS

Not all new Olympic racing events caught on over the years. Three such races were cut after one appearance at the 1900 Games in Paris. One was an obstacle course. Another was called "plunge for distance." In this race, swimmers tried to go as far as they could underwater. The third discarded race was 4,000 meters. That was the longest Olympic swimming race until open-water swimming debuted at the 2008 Games.

BLACK TRAILBLAZERS

Enith Brigitha was born on the Caribbean island of Curaçao. In 1976, while competing for the Netherlands, Brigitha won a pair of Olympic bronze medals. That made her the first Black swimmer to medal at the Games. Historically, access to swimming has been limited for Black people. Brigitha is one of many trailblazing Black stars who broke through on the biggest stage. Anthony Nesty of Suriname became the first Black gold medalist in 1988. Then in 2024, he became the first Black head coach of the US Olympic swim team.

race back-to-back. The men's 4x200-meter freestyle has been contested at every Olympics since 1908. The women's 4x100 freestyle debuted in 1912. Men have since added a 4x100 free, and women now have a 4x200 free. Both men and women also have a 4x100 medley relay. And since the Tokyo Olympics in 2021, men and women compete together in a 4x100 mixed medley relay.

The biggest recent change to the swimming program came at the 2008 Games in Beijing. That year, men and women returned to the open water for a 10-kilometer event. These races are sometimes called marathon swimming.

SWIMMING POWERS

In 1896, just days before his 19th birthday, Gardner Williams became the first American to swim at an Olympic Games. Little is known about how Williams performed in his two races in Athens. His results are officially recorded as "AC," meaning

The United States' Charlie Daniels created the "American crawl," which is one version of the front crawl swimming style.

"also competed." It was not the greatest start for the United States. But before long, the country's swimmers would begin to dominate the sport.

Charlie Daniels was the first great American swimmer. He won five medals, including three golds, at the 1904 Olympics in St. Louis. In 1924, Americans won nine of the 11 swimming gold medals in Paris. That included podium sweeps in three events. By the 1960s, the US team was practically unstoppable. At the 1968 Games in Mexico City, Mexico, Team USA won 52 of the 87 available medals. No other country had more than eight.

A series of superstar swimmers continued the tradition in years to come. Behind elite athletes such as Mark Spitz,

Natalie Coughlin, Michael Phelps, and Katie Ledecky, Americans piled up more than 600 total medals, with around 260 of those being gold, through the 2024 Olympics in Paris. Both totals were more than twice as many as the next-best country's.

Countries such as East Germany, Great Britain, Hungary, and Japan have also enjoyed Olympic swimming success over the years. However, the country that has challenged the

More than 850 swimmers from around the world competed at the 2024 Olympics.

United States the most is Australia. Fanny Durack won the first women's swimming gold medal at the 1912 Olympics. The Aussies topped all countries with 14 total swimming medals on home soil at the 1956 Games in Melbourne. Murray Rose led the way with three golds. Over the years, top athletes such as Dawn Fraser, Ian Thorpe, and Emma McKeon have added to the great Australian swimming tradition.

CHAPTER 3

SETTING THE STANDARD

Ethelda Bleibtrey first started swimming in 1918 to aid her recovery from polio. It turned out the New Yorker was really fast. By 1919, Bleibtrey set her first world record. One year later, at 18, she set five more records while dominating the 1920 Olympics in Antwerp, Belgium. Those Games included only three women's swimming events. Bleibtrey won the 100- and 300-meter freestyle races. Then she anchored the US women's 4x100 freestyle team to win another gold medal. The Americans beat runner-up Great Britain by more than 29 seconds.

Bleibtrey became one of the first Olympic swimming stars. Swimming still wasn't the most welcoming sport to women, though. Before the Olympics, Bleibtrey was arrested for "nude bathing." Her crime was taking off her socks before getting into the water.

Trailblazing competitor Ethelda Bleibtrey of the United States was inducted into the International Swimming Hall of Fame in 1967.

FROM THE OLYMPICS TO HOLLYWOOD

The neighborhood kids never stood a chance against Johnny Weissmuller. Growing up in Chicago, he learned to swim in public pools and Lake Michigan. A local coach noticed how much faster Weissmuller moved than the other kids. Once Weissmuller began serious training, he quickly became one of the sport's all-time greats.

With broad shoulders and muscular arms, Weissmuller powerfully propelled through the water. In 1922, at age 17, he set his first world record. Two years later, he competed in two sports at the 1924 Olympics in Paris. As part of the US men's water polo team, Weissmuller won a bronze medal. But as a swimmer, he proved to be unbeatable.

Weissmuller pulled away from Sweden's Arne Borg, the world-record holder, to win gold in the 400 free. Then he anchored the 4x200 free to an easy win.

DUKE KAHANAMOKU

During the early 1900s, Hawaii-born Duke Kahanamoku used his signature "flutter kick" to become the world's dominant freestyle swimmer. The 1916 Olympics were canceled because of World War I (1914–1918). But competing at the 1912 and 1920 Games, Kahanamoku won four medals. That included back-to-back wins in the 100 free. He also competed in water polo at the 1920 Games. Despite his Olympic success, Kahanamoku is perhaps best known for being a surfer. He also acted in movies for a time.

That set up a showdown with his teammates, the Kahanamoku brothers, in the 100 free. Duke Kahanamoku was the defending Olympic champion. His brother Sam was also an excellent swimmer. But no one was catching Weissmuller. The Americans finished by sweeping the podium, with Weissmuller touching the wall more than two seconds ahead of second-place Duke. The fans in Paris greeted the victory with loud cheers.

Weissmuller returned as one of the most popular athletes at the 1928 Olympics in Amsterdam, Netherlands. And he didn't disappoint, with wins in the 100 and 4x200 free. Years later in

Americans Johnny Weissmuller, *left*, and Duke Kahanamoku, *right*, shake hands during the 1924 Olympics.

1950, sportswriters for the Associated Press voted Weissmuller as the greatest swimmer of the first half of the century. Yet, to many, Weissmuller's swimming was the second most famous part of his life. After retiring, he became a Hollywood actor. From 1930 to 1947, he played Tarzan across 18 films.

WINNING HER WAY

Dawn Fraser could be mischievous, or even rebellious, at times. When she was in the water, though, few people could keep up. As an 18-year-old, Fraser dominated the 1956 Olympics on home soil in Melbourne. She held off countrywoman Lorraine Crapp to win the 100-meter freestyle. Both swam under the world-record time. Fraser finished the Games with another gold in the 4x100 free, plus a silver in the 400 free. The performance made her a superstar in Australia. Then Fraser won three more medals at the 1960 Olympics in Rome, Italy. Among them was another gold in the 100 free.

Some expected Fraser to retire after that. Instead, she decided to compete at the 1964 Olympics in Tokyo. However, in spring that year, Fraser was driving her car when she swerved to avoid an oncoming truck. The car flipped, and the crash killed her mom. Fraser, her sister, and a friend were all injured.

The 1964 Games were just seven months away. Fraser had chipped a bone in her spine. She had to wear a neck brace for

In 1962, Australia's Dawn Fraser became the first woman to swim the 100-meter freestyle in less than one minute.

nine weeks. Doctors warned her that diving into the pool could hurt her neck further. In response, Fraser practiced without diving. The 100 free in Tokyo ended with an all-out sprint to the finish. Fraser held off American teen Sharon Stouder by less than half a second. That made Fraser the first swimmer to win Olympic gold three times in the same event. She also added a silver in the 4x100 free that year.

Fraser might have won even more Olympic medals. However, the Australian federation banned her for 10 years after she and two other athletes were caught stealing a flag during the 1964 Games. Nonetheless, Fraser remained one of Australia's most popular athletes of all time.

SPITZ SETS THE STANDARD

Mark Spitz felt good going into the 1968 Olympics in Mexico City. So when reporters asked how he would do there, the 18-year-old Californian said he would win six gold medals. Instead, he won two golds and four total medals. By any measure that's a successful record. But to Spitz, it was a failure. And to many fans, it served him right for being so cocky.

American Mark Spitz ended his Olympic career with nine golds, one silver, and one bronze.

Spitz learned his lesson about being so outspoken. But his expectations for the 1972 Olympics in Munich were even higher. He wanted to win seven gold medals. That would set a record for a single Olympics. He got off to a strong start in his signature stroke, winning the 200-meter butterfly. Then he won the 200 free, followed by his favorite event, the 100 fly. Along the way, Spitz won two relays as well. Sporting his signature mustache, Spitz grew more famous with each race. But his biggest test was yet to come.

Many expected the 100 free to be Spitz's hardest race. Teammate Jerry Heidenreich had swum the fastest times in the prelims and semifinals. Spitz even considered dropping out before the final. Instead, he raced and beat Heidenreich by nearly half a second. That set up the 4x100 medley to set the record. With Spitz swimming the butterfly leg, Team USA won gold by nearly four seconds.

Four years earlier, Spitz failed to win a single individual event. In Munich, he won four. He also set world records in each of his seven races. It was one of the most incredible Olympic performances in any sport.

A DISPUTED DYNASTY

East German swimmers won six medals at the 1968 Olympics. That marked the beginning of a new sporting dynasty. At the

MATT BIONDI

Matt Biondi only became serious about swimming while in high school. But his natural ability was soon evident. With his massive wingspan, he flew through the water, especially in freestyle races. The Californian won a relay gold medal at age 18 in 1984. Over eight days at the 1988 Games in Seoul, he won seven more medals. Five of those were gold. Biondi added two more golds and a silver at his final Olympics in 1992 in Barcelona, Spain.

next six Summer Games, East Germany often contended for the most medals across all sports. And the country's swimmers were at the forefront.

Roland Matthes won eight medals from 1968 to 1976. That included back-to-back wins in the men's 100- and 200-meter backstroke. With eight medals between 1972 and 1976, Kornelia Ender set a new standard for female swimmers. All four of her gold medals came at the 1976 Games in Montreal. Then, in 1988, Kristen Otto won each of her six finals in Seoul, South Korea. That set a record for most golds by a woman in a single Olympics.

Never were the East German women more dominant than at the 1976 Games. Of the 13 swimming events, they won 11. One of the two they did not win might have been the most memorable. Behind Ender, the East Germans came into the final event, the 4x100 free, as clear favorites. Then Ender put her team up by more than one second after the first leg. Yet by the time Team USA's Shirley Babashoff dove in to start the

East German swimmers combined for 18 total medals in the women's events at the 1976 Games.

fourth leg, the Americans held a slight lead. In a thrilling finish, she held off East Germany's Claudia Hempel for the win.

It was Babashoff's first gold of those Olympics, after previously winning four silvers. The win also gave her some redemption. Many believed the East German teams of this era were using illegal performance-enhancing substances. Babashoff was one of the few who said so directly. Some people called her a bad sport. However, it was later revealed that East Germany had indeed been operating a sophisticated doping scheme. Despite this, its athletes' performances still stand in the record books.

CHAPTER 4

NEXT-LEVEL SWIMMING GREATS

Japan first sent swimmers to the Olympics in 1920. Neither athlete made it out of the heats. So Japanese officials began studying the world's greatest swimmers. They learned what worked well, then tweaked the strokes to make their athletes even faster. At the 1928 Games, a former railway worker named Yoshiyuki Tsuruta won the men's 200-meter breaststroke in Amsterdam. Four years later, Tsuruta defended his Olympic title. His teammate, Reizo Koike, placed second.

Tsuruta's performance helped establish Japan as a great swimming country. Following the 2024 Olympics in Paris, only the United States, Australia, East Germany, and Great Britain had more medals. Japan has proved to be especially strong in the breaststroke events. Kosuke Kitajima showed that in a big way.

Kitajima barely missed a medal at his first Olympics in 2000. The 17-year-old finished fourth in the 100 breaststroke

Along with his seven Olympic medals, Japan's Kosuke Kitajima also won 12 world championship medals.

With nine total medals, including five golds, Ian Thorpe is considered one of Australia's most successful swimmers of all time.

in Sydney. It was one of the last times he missed the podium at a major meet. At the 2004 Games in Athens, Kitajima swept the 100- and 200-meter breaststrokes. Then he won both again in 2008 in Beijing. The last breaststroker to defend a gold medal had been Tsuruta 76 years earlier. Including relays, Kitajima finished with seven medals after competing in his last Olympics in 2012. He also set multiple records along the way.

THORPEDO

At 6-foot-5, Ian Thorpe seemed to fly through the water, propelled by his massive size 17 feet. It was only fitting that the Australian superstar was nicknamed "Thorpedo." Fans knew they were in for something big when Thorpe, at 17, set three world records at Australia's Olympic Trials in 2000.

Racing on home soil in Sydney at the 2000 Games, Thorpe was dominant. In the 400 freestyle, he smashed his own world record to win gold. An hour later, his blazing anchor leg gave Australia a come-from-behind win in the 4x100 freestyle. He later led off the 4x200 free team that won gold with another world record. Thorpe also won a pair of silver medals at those Olympics.

Thorpe's performance made him one of the biggest stars of the 2000 Games. But he had hoped to win another gold in the 200 free. Instead, Pieter van den Hoogenband of the

Netherlands stunned Thorpe and the Australian crowd. The Dutch star also won the 100 free, plus two bronze medals.

Fans were eager for a rematch at the 2004 Olympics in Athens. Then Michael Phelps entered the picture. The American had shown promise as a 15-year-old in Sydney. By Athens, he was a full-blown star looking to win as many as eight gold medals. One of those was in the 200 free. The three-way showdown became known as "The Race of the Century."

Racing outdoors under the bright Greek sun, van den Hoogenband took an early lead. Thorpe, in his bright yellow cap, stuck with him. Phelps was just behind the two leaders at the midway point. Thorpe had already defended his 400 free title in Athens. With one half to go in the 200, Thorpedo struck again. Speeding through the water, he flew past his Dutch rival and surged to victory. Phelps was just behind them in third. Phelps would go on to become the greatest swimmer ever, with

AMERICAN MEN

Michael Phelps was hardly the only US star during the late 1990s and early 2000s. Gary Hall Jr. was one of swimming's great sprinters. He won 10 medals between 1996 and 2004. That included back-to-back wins in the 50 free. Ryan Lochte's 12 medals from 2004 to 2016 tie him for third all-time among swimmers. He shined in the individual medleys. Meanwhile, Caeleb Dressel won nine golds between 2016 and 2024, including five at the Tokyo Games in 2021.

28 Olympic medals. But in "The Race of the Century," Thorpe proved he was still the man to beat.

SUPER LEDECKY

Few people had heard of Katie Ledecky going into the 2012 Olympics in London. After all, the 15-year-old was the youngest

Thorpe, *bottom*, touches the wall to win gold in the 200 freestyle at the 2004 Olympics.

athlete in any sport on the US team that year. She had never raced in a major international meet before.

Ledecky arrived at the Olympics during a bright era for US women. Jenny Thompson had won 12 medals from 1992 to 2004, including eight golds. That stood as the record for a female swimmer until Natalie Coughlin tied it in 2012. But Coughlin's most memorable performance came four years earlier in Beijing. The Californian medaled in all six of

At the 2016 Games in Rio de Janeiro, Brazil, Katie Ledecky of the United States won five medals, including four golds.

From 2016 to 2024, American Simone Manuel won seven Olympic medals, including two golds.

her events. Along the way she became the first woman to defend her Olympic gold medal in the 100 backstroke.

Meanwhile, bubbly 17-year-old Missy Franklin won four gold medals and a bronze at the 2012 Games. That included wins in both individual backstroke events. And at the 2016 Olympics in Rio de Janeiro, Brazil, Simone Manuel won two gold and two silver medals. Tying for first in the 100 free, she became the first Black woman to win an individual swimming gold medal. These swimmers became icons for Team USA. Yet, by the end of her career, Ledecky surpassed them all.

Ledecky's lone event at the 2012 Games was the 800 free. Experts expected Great Britain's Rebecca Adlington to win it.

At the 2024 Games, Ledecky beat her own Olympic-record time in the women's 1,500-meter freestyle during the event final.

Adlington was the defending champion and world-record holder. The hometown fans packed the London Aquatics Center to cheer her on. Instead, Ledecky sped to an early lead and never looked back. She just missed breaking Adlington's world record. But she'd have it soon. And before long, she would dominate the distance freestyle events.

At the 2024 Olympics in Paris, Ledecky claimed her fourth consecutive gold medal in the 800 free. That made her only the seventh Olympian to four-peat in a single event. But her most dominant performance was in the 1,500 free, where she won by 10.33 seconds. Two additional medals that summer brought her career medal total to 14, nine of them being gold. Ledecky left Paris as the most decorated Olympic female swimmer of all time.

TEAM USA VS THE WORLD

Team USA has long dominated Olympic swimming. But other countries are catching up. Never was that truer than at the 2024 Games. That summer, Frenchman Leon Marchand thrilled the hometown fans with four gold medals in four individual races. Two of those gold medals came on the same night, which was the first time a swimmer had ever done that. Meanwhile, in her second Olympics, 17-year-old Canadian Summer McIntosh won three individual gold medals and a silver. That included a sweep of the IM races.

The big question, though, was whether Australia could finally unseat Team USA in the gold-medal chase. In the previous eight Olympics, American swimmers had come out on top. But the Aussies got off to

AGELESS WONDER

Dara Torres was known for her legendary comebacks. The Californian won four swimming medals across three Olympics from 1984 to 1992. After retiring to become a model, she returned to the Games in 2000 to win five more medals. Then she retired again, only to come back once more for the 2008 Games. At age 41, Torres became the oldest woman to swim at the Olympics. She also won three silver medals.

France's Leon Marchand was trained by Bob Bowman, Michael Phelps's former coach, for the 2024 Olympics.

a strong start in Paris. Ariarne Titmus held off McIntosh and Ledecky in an epic women's 400 freestyle race on the opening day. In the coming days, Kaylee McKeown swept the women's backstroke events. Cameron McEvoy and Mollie O'Callaghan added golds in the men's 50 free and women's 200 free, respectively. The Aussies also won two golds in the women's relay events. With one day to go, Australia led all countries with seven swimming gold medals. Team USA trailed with six.

Then, Bobby Finke dove into the pool. The US distance star took an early lead in the men's 1,500 free. Lap after lap, he never let up. Finally, in world-record time, Finke touched the wall first. It was his third Olympic gold medal, after winning

From left, Australia's Lani Pallister, Ariarne Titmus, Brianna Throssell, and Mollie O'Callaghan celebrate winning the women's 4x200 freestyle relay in Olympic-record time at the 2024 Games.

the 800 and 1,500 free at the Tokyo Games in 2021. It also marked the first individual medal for the US men in Paris. But most importantly for the Americans, it tied them with Australia for the most golds.

It all came down to the women's 4x100 medley. This time, it wasn't close. The team of Regan Smith, Lilly King, Gretchen Walsh, and Torri Huske won gold in world-record time. Australia finished in second. As had often been the case in Olympic swimming, Team USA swimmers proved once again that they were the biggest stars of the pool.

GLOSSARY

anchor
The last competitor for a team in a relay.

debut
First appearance.

doping
Using illegal substances to boost one's performance.

dynasty
A team that has an extended period of success, usually winning multiple championships in the process.

lap
One trip to the other end of the pool.

leg
A portion of a race.

polio
An infectious disease that attacks the brain and spinal cord, often of young children.

preliminary
An early round of a competition in which the top finishers move on.

protest
A formal challenge to a result.

rival
An opponent with whom a player or team has a fierce and ongoing competition.

split
A swimmer's individual time in a relay race.

sweep
When one country wins all three medals in an event.

wingspan
The distance between the tips of people's fingers when holding their arms straight out to each side.

MORE INFORMATION

BOOKS

Buckley, James, Jr. *Who Is Katie Ledecky?* Penguin Workshop, 2024.

Gitlin, Marty. *Olympic Swimming and Diving Legends*. Black Rabbit, 2021.

Price, Karen. *GOATs of Olympic Sports*. Abdo, 2022.

ONLINE RESOURCES

To learn more about Olympic swimming, please visit **abdobooklinks.com** or scan this QR code. These links are routinely monitored and updated to provide the most current information available.

INDEX

Australia, 4, 7, 12, 19, 23, 28–29, 34, 37–38, 43–45

Babashoff, Shirley, 32–33
Biondi, Matt, 32
Bleibtrey, Ethelda, 24
Brigitha, Enith, 20

Čavić, Milorad, 10–12
Coubertin, Pierre de, 14
Coughlin, Natalie, 22, 40–41
Cseh, László, 4, 8–9

Daniels, Charlie, 21
Dressel, Caeleb, 38

East Germany, 22, 31–33, 34
Ender, Kornelia, 32

Finke, Bobby, 44
Franklin, Missy, 41
Fraser, Dawn, 23, 28–29

Great Britain, 22, 24, 34, 41

Hajós, Alfréd, 16
Hall, Gary, Jr., 38

Kahanamoku, Duke, 26–27
Kitajima, Kosuke, 34, 37

Ledecky, Katie, 22, 39–44
Lezak, Jason, 7–8, 13
Lochte, Ryan, 4, 6, 38

Manuel, Simone, 41
Marchand, Leon, 43
McIntosh, Summer, 43–44

Nesty, Anthony, 20

Phelps, Michael, 4–13, 22, 38

Spitz, Mark, 4, 10, 12, 21, 30–31
strokes, 4, 6, 18–19, 31–32, 34, 37, 41, 44

Thorpe, Ian, 23, 37–39
Torres, Dara, 43
Tsuruta, Yoshiyuki, 34, 37

van den Hoogenband, Pieter, 37–38

Weissmuller, Johnny, 26–28
Williams, Gardner, 20

ABOUT THE AUTHOR

Chrös McDougall is a sportswriter, author, and book editor who focuses on Olympic and Paralympic sports. At the 2021 Olympics in Tokyo, he covered the men's 1,500-meter freestyle race, when Team USA's Bobby Finke became the first US winner of that event in 37 years. McDougall lives in Minneapolis, Minnesota, with his wife, two children, and a boxer who doesn't much like to swim named Eira.